The Challenges and Opportunities of Institutional Capacity Building Through Professional Military Education

Lessons from the Defense Education Enhancement Program

TREVOR JOHNSTON, ALAN G. STOLBERG

Prepared for the Defense Security Cooperation Agency
Approved for public release; distribution unlimited

 NATIONAL DEFENSE RESEARCH INSTITUTE

For more information on this publication, visit **www.rand.org/t/RRA1238-1**.

About RAND

The RAND Corporation is a research organization that develops solutions to public policy challenges to help make communities throughout the world safer and more secure, healthier and more prosperous. RAND is nonprofit, nonpartisan, and committed to the public interest. To learn more about RAND, visit www.rand.org.

Research Integrity

Our mission to help improve policy and decisionmaking through research and analysis is enabled through our core values of quality and objectivity and our unwavering commitment to the highest level of integrity and ethical behavior. To help ensure our research and analysis are rigorous, objective, and nonpartisan, we subject our research publications to a robust and exacting quality-assurance process; avoid both the appearance and reality of financial and other conflicts of interest through staff training, project screening, and a policy of mandatory disclosure; and pursue transparency in our research engagements through our commitment to the open publication of our research findings and recommendations, disclosure of the source of funding of published research, and policies to ensure intellectual independence. For more information, visit www.rand.org/about/research-integrity.

RAND's publications do not necessarily reflect the opinions of its research clients and sponsors.

Published by the RAND Corporation, Santa Monica, Calif.
© 2022 RAND Corporation
RAND® is a registered trademark.

Library of Congress Cataloging-in-Publication Data is available for this publication.

ISBN: 978-1-9774-0937-9

Cover: Photo by Public Affairs Office, Baltic Defence College.

About This Report

This report is intended to provide a program update on the status of the Defense Education Enhancement Program (DEEP). The principal audience of this report includes U.S., North Atlantic Treaty Organization (NATO), and partner nation personnel involved in DEEP country programs. This report also discusses recent program challenges and identifies opportunities for continued growth and improvement. For institutional capacity building (ICB) practitioners, this report also offers more-general lessons on how professional military education can support other efforts to encourage institutional change and development. For the broader U.S. security cooperation enterprise, which comprises a rich and diverse community of U.S. Department of Defense military and civilian personnel across different agencies and offices around the world, this report can offer insights into the practical challenges of conducting assessment, monitoring, and evaluation for ICB and associated defense education programs, which often focus on slow-to-change institutions and structures.

RAND National Security Research Division

This research was sponsored by the Defense Security Cooperation Agency and conducted within the Forces and Resources Policy Center of the RAND National Security Research Division (NSRD), which operates the National Defense Research Institute (NDRI), a federally funded research and development center sponsored by the Office of the Secretary of Defense, the Joint Staff, the Unified Combatant Commands, the Navy, the Marine Corps, the defense agencies, and the defense intelligence enterprise.

For more information on the RAND Forces and Resources Policy Center, see www.rand.org/nsrd/frp or contact the director (contact information is provided on the webpage).

Acknowledgments

We thank the Defense Security Cooperation Agency for sponsoring RAND NDRI's support to the NATO DEEP. We also thank the Institute for Security Governance for its support in this work and helpful feedback on this report. We thank the many DEEP officers and academic leads—past and present—who generously gave us their time, offering critical insights through interviews and providing feedback throughout the research process.

We thank our reviewers, Charles Goldman and John Berry, who provided exceptional comments and suggestions that greatly improved this report. We also thank our RAND colleagues Susan Sohler Everingham and Jennifer Moroney for their useful suggestions, feedback, and comments that helped develop this report. We also thank John Winkler and Molly McIntosh of the Forces and Resources Policy Center within RAND NDRI for their support throughout the project. All errors of fact and interpretation remain those of the authors.

Summary

In this report, we summarize lessons from the RAND Corporation's work supporting the Defense Education Enhancement Program (DEEP). Established in 2007 as a joint effort of the North Atlantic Treaty Organization (NATO) International Staff and the Partnership for Peace Consortium (PfPC), DEEP supports institutional capacity building (ICB) through curriculum development, faculty development, and institutional support to partner schools.

We provide an update on program efforts conducted between January 2018 and December 2020 and discuss some of the major challenges in program execution and potential drivers of success. During this period, DEEP grew in scope and enjoyed some significant successes while having to navigate unprecedented challenges amid the coronavirus disease 2019 (COVID-19) pandemic.

Research Approach

Our analysis and findings draw on various sources, including DEEP country program strategic plans, which describe objectives and planned activities for each country; annual monitoring and evaluation reports; after-action reports drafted by individual country leads or subject-matter experts following executed activities; aggregated event activity data; a series of semistructured key informant interviews with past and present DEEP officers and academic leads; and a robust secondary literature, including media reports and academic and policy studies.

Using these sources, we explore program challenges and drivers of success. Although this analysis draws broadly on the experiences and lessons from the entire program, we focus our discussion on three cases: those in Armenia, Tunisia, and Ukraine. We trace program evolution across these three cases, exploring how DEEP officers managed resistant stakeholders, institutional constraints, and structural challenges.

Key Findings and Observations

From Disruption to Innovation: Increasing Efficiency Through Distance Learning

The COVID-19 pandemic brought about a steep learning curve for both providers and partners, introducing both technological and pedagogical challenges. DEEP used virtual engagements to replace, albeit imperfectly, a wide variety of in-person activities and events, including initial site survey scoping visits, annual country program reviews, faculty development workshops, curriculum development workshops, and even large conference meetings. Although initially disruptive, the pandemic ultimately resulted in academic innovation, greater programmatic agility, cost savings, and efficiency gains that can be sustained after pandemic-related travel restrictions end.

Partner Interests and Institutional Constraints: Building Trust Through Collaboration

Local institutional constraints, such as course length or degree requirements, at professional military education (PME) schools can initially result in a poor match between DEEP efforts and the needs of the PME institution, creating challenges in program design. When leadership at local PME institutions resist program efforts, it is incumbent on DEEP officers to work with partners to tailor efforts to specific partner needs and to encourage local ownership. These challenges can normally be overcome by leveraging the collective expertise of NATO-allied provider schools, many of which have specialization in different areas of warfighting. Although such collaboration can yield a better match between institutional needs and program design, it comes at a cost, requiring more time and effort to experiment with new approaches to curriculum or faculty development.

Diverse Needs and Requirements: Flexibility and Resilience Through a Multinational Approach

As a joint effort between NATO and the PfPC, DEEP was built on a multinational approach, which offers greater flexibility in matching partners with a more-diverse variety of providers. This approach allows partner countries to be paired with providers with whom they might be more comfortable because of a shared language, culture, or history. Macro-structural challenges in a partner military, such as a long history of Soviet/Russian military practice, can limit potential opportunities and require programs to work around entrenched systems. Such flexibility critically depends on a provider having the capacity and interest to support a request. ICB efforts like defense education support often take years to achieve effects and could depend on broader political or structural changes. These efforts have the potential to stimulate enduring improvements in partner militaries but require strategic presence and patience.

Hard and Slow to Change: Increasing Returns on Investment Through Strategic Patience

Under the best of conditions, ICB efforts often take years to achieve effects and could ultimately depend on broader political or structural changes. These changes can come suddenly and without warning, making it difficult for program officers to predict or plan for such opportunities. But one thing is clear: Seizing these opportunities requires presence and patience. Partners' complicated political and personal interests often underlie these obstacles to progress, and time is key to better understanding these interests. Winning over partner nation Ministry of Defense and general staff leaders, as well as PME school staffs, is critical to program success but depends on strong relationships built over years. DEEP efforts have been most effective when there is programmatic consistency and continuity in the personnel, which can help overcome stakeholder resistance. In most cases, academic leads and program managers typically work for years with the same country and partner school leaders and faculty. Sustained engagement can help grow trust and familiarity over time, allowing program officers to seize opportunities when they arise.

Contents

Figures and Table

Figures

Table

CHAPTER ONE

Introduction

Established in 2007 through a combined effort by the North Atlantic Treaty Organization (NATO) International Staff and the Partnership for Peace Consortium (PfPC), the Defense Education Enhancement Program (DEEP) "is one of the core elements of the [NATO] Defense and Related Security Capacity Building [DCB] initiative" and is intended to help "build defense capacity and interoperability" (NATO International Staff, 2019b). DEEP supports these institutional capacity building (ICB) objectives by providing assistance in modern curriculum development (what to teach), faculty development (how to teach), and institutional support (administration and management) for NATO partner professional military education (PME) schools (NATO International Staff, 2019b).[1] Program execution and coordination are conducted jointly by the NATO International Staff and the PfPC.

A unique feature of DEEP is its multinational approach to security cooperation. Before DEEP, there were no U.S. or NATO security cooperation programs specifically designed to support long-term efforts that focused on defense education. DEEP offers an assistance mechanism to help professionalize partner nation schools while also supporting efforts to sustain other U.S. and allied ICB programs for security sector ministries and general, joint, and service staffs. DEEP complements these other efforts by providing partner schools with faculty training and curriculum development in functional areas that are often the focus of ICB, such as policy, strategy, planning, logistics, and human resources. This complementarity supports long-term sustainment of these related ICB efforts.

This report builds on analysis and observations documented in an earlier RAND Corporation publication, *Building Partner-Nation Capacity Through the Defense Education Enhancement Program*, which presents an assessment of DEEP efforts though the end of 2017 (Stolberg, Johnson, and Kupe, 2018). In addition to providing an update on program efforts between January 2018 and December 2020, we discuss some of the major challenges to program execution and potential drivers of success. Drawing on lessons learned during the past two years, including the challenges of executing efforts during the coronavirus disease 2019

---

[1] The DCB Initiative component of ICB "helps partners improve their defence and related security capacities, as well as their resilience. . . . It can include various types of support, ranging from strategic advice on defence and security sector reform and institution-building, to development of local forces through education and training, or advice and assistance in specialised areas such as logistics or cyber defence" (as quoted in NATO, 2021).

(COVID-19) pandemic, we provide recommendations for increasing program efficiency; maximizing effectiveness; and improving assessment, monitoring, and evaluation (AM&E).[2]

This report is intended to inform U.S. personnel, NATO Allies, and other Euro-Atlantic governments of the DEEP's status, its opportunities and challenges, and ways the program can be improved. For ICB practitioners, this report also offers more general-lessons on how PME can support other efforts to encourage institutional change and development. For the broader U.S. security cooperation enterprise, which comprises a rich and diverse community of U.S. Department of Defense (DoD) military and civilian personnel across different agencies and offices around the world, this report can offer insights into the practical challenges of conducting AM&E for ICB and associated defense education programs, which tend to focus on slow-to-change institutions and structures.

Research Methods and Limitations

Although this report draws broadly on experiences and lessons from all DEEP efforts, much of our analysis focuses on three illustrative cases in Armenia, Tunisia, and Ukraine. We selected these cases because they vary in terms of program age, scope, number of activities, and focus area (e.g., curricula topics). In choosing our cases, we tried to strike a balance among these criteria to help tease out lessons and findings that could apply more broadly. Collectively, these cases can offer valuable insights into some of the core challenges that DEEP efforts face, including stakeholder politics, PME institutional constraints, and structural legacies.

Drawing on a mixed-methods approach, we trace program evolution through these cases and describe the conditions under which DEEP efforts can navigate these challenges. Our analysis leverages a variety of data and documents, including official planning materials, annual AM&E reports, program activity and event data, after-action reports (AARs), official correspondence, secondary sources (e.g., academic studies and think tank reports), and key informant interviews.[3] These interviews—which were with NATO and PfPC staff, DEEP officers, and academic leads—provided firsthand, inside accounts of the challenges that DEEP efforts face and were essential to tracing the evolution of country programs over time. (Unless otherwise indicated, all mentions of interviews refer to author interviews with these individuals. These interviews occurred between September and December 2020.)

---

[2] All data related to the Ukraine DEEP case study were collected and analyzed prior to the 24 February 2022 Russian invasion. The attack on Ukraine did not result in any changed observations or conclusions in report findings.

[3] All interviews are attributed anonymously throughout this report in compliance with the U.S. Federal Policy for the Protection of Human Subjects (also known as the Common Rule). Furthermore, human subject protections (HSP) protocols have been used in this report in accordance with the appropriate statutes and DoD regulations that govern HSP. The views of the interviewees, which HSP rendered anonymously, are solely their own and do not represent the official policy or position of DoD, U.S. Intelligence Community agencies, or the U.S. government.

Our data collection effort omits a critical perspective. This study was conducted during the COVID-19 pandemic, which severely limited the research team's ability to travel; made it difficult to conduct interviews; and all but precluded direct engagement with partner PME administrative staff, instructors, students, and military or civilian officials. Although interviews with U.S. and NATO personnel can provide invaluable insights into the challenges that programs face during program planning and execution, these accounts offer, at best, an incomplete picture. They fail to fully capture the distinct perspective that partners can provide, including the ways in which programs do or do not meet the needs of PME students, institutions, or partner militaries. We should note, however, that like any interview subject, partners might have their own interests (e.g., incentives to exaggerate program success to secure future funding), which can introduce bias. Despite this concern, partner perspectives are important to the broader story, making their omission a limitation to our analysis.

Organization of the Report

The remainder of this report proceeds as follows. In Chapter Two, we begin with an overview of the program's structure and activities, including its annual strategic plans and AM&E process, followed by a description of developments since 2018. In Chapter Three, we discuss program challenges and drivers of success across Armenia, Tunisia, and Ukraine. Following these case studies, Chapter Four then offers a broader discussion of lessons learned and best practices identified during the past three years as the program adapted to remote and distance-based learning during a global pandemic. Finally, in Chapter Five, we summarize some of our major findings and offer a series of recommendations for improving program effectiveness, efficiency, and impact.

CHAPTER TWO

Program Structure, Objectives, and Recent Efforts

In this chapter, we review DEEP's structure and objectives, including the program's AM&E. After summarizing the program's general structure, we reconstruct a notional theory of change for DEEP, describing how program efforts are expected to result in different kinds of outcomes.[1] Finally, we conclude with a brief analysis of the key DEEP initiatives and efforts that were conducted from 2018 through 2020 as the program continued to expand to other NATO partner countries and schools.

Program Structure and Objectives

Since its inception in 2007, DEEP has centered on three core features: providing ICB for defense education institutions, creating programs that will support the sustainment of other U.S. and allied ICB programs, and ensuring that multinational NATO-standard approaches are tailored for individual partner country and school programs by multinational expert teams. All three features guide defense education security cooperation support for NATO partner nations (NATO International Staff, 2019b).

DEEP is open to any nation defined by NATO as a *partner country*. This includes Partnership for Peace countries that are members of the Euro-Atlantic Partnership Council (e.g., Armenia and Ukraine), NATO's Mediterranean Dialogue nations (e.g., Mauritania and Tunisia), NATO Istanbul Cooperation Initiative countries (e.g., Kuwait), and the NATO "partners across the globe" framework (e.g., Iraq) (NATO, 2020).

DEEP helps modernize and professionalize NATO partner defense education institutions, typically categorized as PME schools, which include war colleges at the strategic level of war, staff colleges at the operational level of war, military academies that commission new junior officers, and noncommissioned officer (NCO) academies that educate and train

---

[1] In 2018, DEEP did not have an explicit theory of change. The theory that we describe in this chapter is a reconstruction of the underlying logic derived from program materials and interviews with program officers.

junior leaders at the tactical level of war.[2] DEEP also supports other schools that educate and train partner forces (e.g., junior officer training courses, English language training schools, and Ministry of Defense [MOD] schools that train both civilian and military ministerial staff personnel).[3]

This support is provided in three general functional defense education capacity building areas: curriculum development (what to teach), faculty development (how to teach), and institutional support (school administration and management). *Curriculum development* supports the creation of new courses, individual lessons, and their application to either resident or nonresident online instruction. These efforts have also supported the development of reference curricula, which offer value to program managers and academic leads alike (NATO International Staff, 2019b). Since 2008, seven reference curricula have been published and made available to DEEP partner nations.[4] The new Counterterrorism Reference Curriculum has already been employed in two different schools in Ukraine and will be the first reference curriculum converted into a distance learning/online curriculum format (Stolberg, 2020b).

Complementing this curriculum development, DEEP also focuses on *faculty development*, which provides training for partner school faculty on modern teaching methods. These engagements often take the form of short courses, which comprise a series of multiple-day workshops. The intent is for the partner school instructor to be able to apply active learning approaches, modern assessment techniques, and curriculum design in a student-centric learning environment. At the conclusion of these workshops, the DEEP expert team working with the partner school leadership will typically identify the best students in the initial workshops who will have an opportunity to participate in the DEEP Master Instructor Program (MIP). Identified collaboratively by the DEEP faculty development team and the partner school leadership, the students admitted into the MIP program should have had previous participation in the DEEP faculty Foundation Development Program, have perceived capacity to educate their own faculty on the basics of current adult learning principles and best practices, and have a minimum of two years remaining on the school faculty.[5] The MIP program prepares these individuals to serve as the partner school experts in modern teaching

---

[2] All types of described schools are identified in NATO International Staff, 2019b; PfPC, 2020c; and PfPC Education Development Working Group [EDWG], 2020c.

[3] Limited English language skills is a common but critically important challenge for DEEP and other ICB programs. Drawing on U.S. and NATO doctrine and pedagogical tools often requires working-level English, which can be a major barrier for some partner administrators, instructors, and students.

[4] Reference curricula include Partnership Action Plan for Defense Institution Building (PAP-DIB); Generic Officer Professional Military Education; NCO Professional Military Education; Cyber Security; Counterinsurgency (COIN); Building Integrity (BI); and Counterterrorism. For more details, see PfPC and NATO International Staff, 2020.

[5] For a detailed description of all desired DEEP prerequisites for MIP program participation, see PfPC EDWG Educators Faculty Development Group, 2021.

methods and to conduct their own faculty development training programs for their school's instructors without external support (PfPC EDWG, 2020b).

The final focus area in DEEP is *institutional support*—assisting partners in administering and managing PME institutions. DEEP providers share best practices and lessons learned from their own experiences in managing military schools and academies, helping partner leaders identify specific ways in which they can improve their systems. This sharing can go both ways, with providers also learning from partners (e.g., Ukrainian officers provided NATO with insights from their experience fighting against Russian irregular warfare). These exchanges are often conducted in country but can also include visits to NATO countries. In one such example, a delegation from Ukraine's National Defence University (NDU) visited the U.S. NDU to discuss faculty professionalization, the development of a modern library system, the advantages of a wargaming center, and the value of a research center (Magalotti, 2016).

DEEP's unique multinational approach to security cooperation has myriad implications for program planning, resourcing, and execution. Although this approach offers distinct advantages (e.g., burden-sharing), it can also introduce complications (e.g., need for coordination). DEEP efforts depend on the cooperative planning, funding, and execution of events via a coordinated effort by the NATO International Staff and PfPC. These program efforts are broadly aligned with U.S. geographic combatant command country objectives and NATO Integrated Partnership Action Plans.

DEEP is intended to complement and help sustain other national ICB programs and efforts. ICB efforts often focus on higher levels and organizations, such as security sector ministries and joint, general, or service staffs. Capacity gains made at these levels might be fragile and can erode over time if not built on a foundation that supports these changes. DEEP efforts could help establish such a foundation. As seen in program support for the Defence Management School in Ukraine and the Ministerial Training and Development College in Iraq, DEEP efforts might be able to complement other ICB programs by training MOD personnel, both civilians and military, in areas like planning and critical thinking skills (Stolberg, 2020b).

Program Planning and AM&E

Historically, the program assessment process has been based on DEEP experts' qualitative observations of partner-nation school activities, their discussions with partner-nation counterparts, and their subject-matter expertise (PfPC EDWG, 2016), broadly framed around eight categories.[6] In an effort to refine and more rigorously capture these assessments, in late 2019, DEEP began incorporating specific, measurable, achievable, relevant, and time-bound

---

[6] These categories are adoption of modern PME, academic structures and degree requirement, inclusion of modern subject matter into course curricula to include development of entirely new courses, adoption of modern teaching methodologies by PME faculty, adoption of NCO education support of senior partner-nation and defense education institution leadership for DEEP efforts, contribution of partner-nation educa-

(SMART) objectives into its planning process (McNerney et al., 2016).[7] These SMART objectives are intended to improve program design, execution, and monitoring and evaluation. These processes critically depend on identifying *specific* objectives for an individual event or project. Developing more *measurable* objectives supports better monitoring and performance plans, which in turn can allow for more rigorous evaluations over time. However, these efforts must set realistic expectations and have *achievable* goals in mind. In addition, requiring that objectives are *relevant* helps ensure that program efforts remain in support of U.S. and NATO policy goals. Finally, designing *time-bound* objectives can help encourage efficiency and accountability.

A newly refined SMART framework has already been incorporated into select 2020 DEEP country program strategic plans. Based on partner school support requests, these strategic plans are collaboratively developed for each DEEP country and updated annually by the PfPC and NATO program managers and DEEP country academic leads. They are then transmitted to the Office of the Secretary of Defense (OSD), the Defense Security Cooperation Agency, the geographic combatant commands, and respective U.S. embassy country teams for comment and input. One such example from Tunisia follows (PfPC, 2020b):

- **Specific:** Facilitate faculty (1) adaptation of modern andragogy learning styles, journaling, and Bloom's taxonomy (hierarchical ordering of cognitive skills used to design curriculum) and (2) employment of active learning to facilitate a seminar; develop and adapt case studies as a curriculum tool; and apply modern lesson plan developmental techniques, including assessment, monitoring, and evaluation.
- **Measurable:** At the conclusion of a multihour course over the span of 1–2 one-week workshops, student faculty will be able to (1) utilize modern learning styles, journaling, and Bloom's taxonomy (2) and employ active learning to facilitate a seminar; develop and adapt case studies as a curriculum tool; and use modern lesson plan developmental techniques, including AM&E, without external support.
- **Achievable:** The MOD and school leadership support the war college instructors' teaching with modern teaching methods. The faculty are motivated to learn. The PfPC budget is in place. European and U.S. academic provider experts are qualified and available. All indications are that basic faculty development can be developed in the next 12 months (subject to COVID-19-related virtual and in-person workshop scheduling).
- **Relevant:** The ability to instruct with modern teaching methods will permit the faculty to emphasize critical thinking skills for the future operational or strategic leader student body, a key component for NATO interoperability.

---

tors and NCO experts (military and civilian) in DEEP efforts, contribution to strategic goals, and contribution to meeting partner requirements and goals. See Stolberg, Johnson, and Kupe, 2018.

[7] This proposal was approved by the PfPC's Consultative Steering Committee on November 14, 2019. See PfPC, 2019.

- **Time bound:** Basic faculty development support should be concluded in 12 months, subject to COVID-19-related virtual and in-person workshop scheduling, when the instructors are able to employ modern teaching methods to deliver curricula.

Other examples of SMART objectives in DEEP strategic plans include curriculum development for Building Integrity courses at four Armenian PME schools and a graduate-level NATO logistics course from Ukraine's NDU (PfPC, 2020f; PfPC, 2020g).

Theory of Change

The overarching goal of DEEP is to encourage the leadership and faculty of partner schools to modernize and professionalize what and how they teach in accordance with NATO standards. The program's notional general theory of change is illustrated in Figure 2.1,[8] which maps program *inputs* to discrete *outputs*, which can lead to bigger *outcomes* that might have

FIGURE 2.1
DEEP Notional Theory of Change

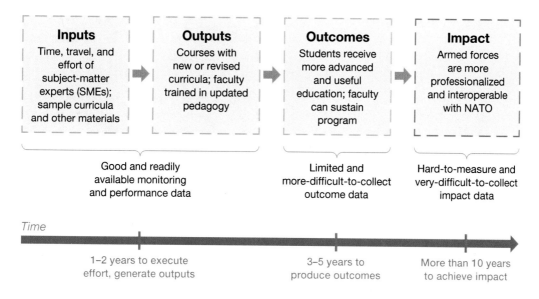

NOTE: The color-coding captures the relative difficulty of data collection, with green being the most accessible and red the most challenging.

---

[8] A theory of change is "intended to make implicit assumptions more explicit, which describes why certain actions will produce a desired change in a given context, and clearly states what the intended outcome of the initiative will be and how it will be achieved." See Office of the Under Secretary of Defense for Policy, 2017.

a broader *impact* over time. We discuss each of these terms, providing concrete examples and describing the data requirements and related challenges associated with program AM&E.[9]

Inputs are the essential resources used to plan and execute program efforts, such as "funding, manpower, and expertise" (Office of the Under Secretary of Defense for Policy, 2017). In the DEEP context, these inputs typically include (1) the time and effort of SMEs who travel to meet with partners, plan and conduct program activities, and provide additional support and guidance between visits or events and (2) instructional resources and other materials, such as sample curricula, that partners use to build or revise curricula or develop their pedagogy. Specific examples include three multiday workshops supporting the Basic Faculty Development program for Ukraine's Zhytomyr Military Institute of Technology (ZMIT) (PfPC, 2020h), multinational workshops to develop a joint planning course for the Tunisian war college (NATO International Staff, 2019a), and a series of training workshops for faculty to become master instructors at the Armenian V. Sargsyan Military University (VSMU) (PfPC, 2020i).

Outputs are the near-term results of program efforts and are defined in the security cooperation context as "a deliverable or product, good, or service directly resulting from a security cooperation initiative or activity, such as the number of training events and the number of unit members trained" (Office of the Under Secretary of Defense for Policy, 2017). In the case of DEEP, these outputs might include courses using new or revised curricula and faculty trained in updated pedagogy. Assuming the partner school permits a degree of transparency, these outputs can be readily determined by reviewing written curricula and catalog course offerings and confirmed through classroom observation. Specific examples include faculty now using modern curriculum design, Bloom's taxonomy (Heick, 2020), and active teaching methods at Ukraine's ZMIT (PfPC, 2020e); the development and delivery of a new NATO-standard Joint Operational Planning and Decision Making course at the Tunisian war college (PfPC, 2020d); and the growing number of instructors that trained in the MIP at Armenia's VSMU (PfPC, 2020d).

Outcomes represent longer-term results of program efforts, which derive from "cumulative effects of interventions over time," and, with respect to security cooperation, seek to change everything from partner behavior and policy to overall capabilities and capacity (Office of the Under Secretary of Defense for Policy, 2017). Often, the distinction between outputs and outcomes can be somewhat muddled in practice, but in the DEEP context, the major outcomes tend to focus on improving the overall educational experience for students and building the capacity of a school and its faculty to help sustain program gains without external support. Evaluating outcomes is more difficult than evaluating outputs because it not only requires greater access to partner schools and students but also can entail more abstract indicators that might be harder to measure. Examples of potential outcomes include students at Ukraine's ZMIT receiving modern critical thinking–based instruction, Arme-

---

[9] For more on the value of theory of change and logic model in security cooperation AM&E, see Marquis et al., 2016.

nian master instructors at VSMU who can sustain training in modern teaching methods for their own teaching cadre, and the students at the Tunisian war college receiving instruction in joint operational planning that aligns with NATO standards.

Over time, program outcomes might contribute to and have a broader impact on partner systems. Among the components of a theory of change, impact can be the hardest to define and measure, because it often relates to more-fundamental changes in structures or institutions. Such change depends not only on the success of the program but also on a series of conditions that align with, support, and complement program efforts. In the case of DEEP, the long-term potential impact of program efforts extends beyond the school and its faculty in a partner's armed forces. By focusing on a partner's core PME institutions, DEEP efforts can have far-reaching effects, spanning the armed services. PME graduates' ability to apply learned information and such processes as leadership techniques, operational planning approaches, staff procedures, and doctrinal concepts can help professionalize a partner nation's military and inculcate NATO standards and procedures. As the number of PME graduates grows over time and proliferates throughout the force, we might be able to see an operational impact, resulting in greater interoperability with NATO or other modern militaries.

Given the time it can take to achieve such an impact, it can be hard to find clear examples of how DEEP efforts translate into operational effects on the ground. One such example comes from Kazakhstan, where DEEP supported the Kazakh Partnership Training and Education Centres. Between 2013 and 2016, DEEP assisted in the development of four courses for the institution's faculty: UN Staff Operations, Legal Aspects of Peace Support Operations, UN Protection of Civilians, and UN Military Experts on Mission. According to one DEEP officer, these courses helped Kazakh officers to develop the capacity to deploy on UN peacekeeping missions for the first time in the country's history (PfPC, 2016b). After these initial missions in Africa and Haiti in 2015 and 2016, a Kazakh infantry company deployed to Lebanon in 2018 (PfPC, 2020a). Given time and resources, a similar impact could be made on the Tunisian armed forces, who have made peacekeeping missions an initial focus of their DEEP efforts.

In terms of measuring impact, it is difficult to collect data that can clearly attribute a direct relationship between what was learned in a specific course and how it was applied in an operational setting. Only former students would be able to determine how the information obtained in the classroom was applied in a follow-on operational environment. To varying degrees, a former student might be influenced by certain personal biases that could affect analysis of that linkage. This bias could stem from liking or not liking a course or a course instructor or from the ability to remember certain curriculum details that might be directly relevant to the operational mission.

Even if we could accurately capture the degree to which a course provided useful information in an operational setting, the question of impact relates to broader effects, requiring many cumulative effects and favorable conditions to align. Measuring these effects over time and controlling for such conditions is extremely difficult, making it all but impossible to rigorously evaluate the long-term impact of any PME program.

Recent Program Efforts and Activities

Having described the program's overall structure and objectives, we now briefly discuss DEEP efforts between 2018 and 2020. During this period, DEEP was largely stable, with some modest growth. As of December 2020, there were 17 active DEEP country programs,[10] which represent a net increase of four countries since 2017. During this time, new programs began in Bosnia and Herzegovina, Morocco, and Jordan, and the Iraq program was reinitiated in 2019.

Although admittedly coarse, event data can provide a useful summary of program efforts over time. Figure 2.2 shows a plot of DEEP events by year and funding source from 2018 through 2020. The stacked bar chart shows the total number of events per year, disaggregating among three types of funding: NATO DEEP funds (the yellow bar), PfPC funds (the red bar), and cofunding from both DEEP and PfPC (the blue bar). The data are a combination of NATO and PfPC sources.

The figure gives a rough sense of DEEP activity from 2018 through 2020. From 2018 to 2019, DEEP events increased by 35 percent, with the gains entirely driven by NATO-funded events. Not surprisingly, given the disruption from the COVID-19 outbreak, 2020 saw a significant decline compared with 2019, with program officers forced to cancel or postpone many of their planned engagements. This reduction is especially pronounced among PfPC-funded events, which saw a 61 percent decrease from 2019 to 2020.

Here we should note that NATO and the PfPC count events differently, which can make direct comparisons somewhat fraught. The PfPC, in line with more-standard U.S. event-tracking procedures, includes only events that are funded with the explicit purpose of executing DEEP support activities (e.g., curriculum development workshops, faculty development workshops, and institutional support workshops). NATO data tracking, by contrast, includes some events that are related to DEEP but are not exclusively funded with these objectives in mind (e.g., support for partner students to attend NATO-allied courses or training). These accounting practices are important because they result in different numerical depictions of events and could inflate the relative number of NATO events. Despite these differences in

---

[10] The full list of countries and their (re)initiation years are as follows: Afghanistan (est. 2010), Armenia (est. 2009), Azerbaijan (est. 2010), Bosnia and Herzegovina (est. 2019), Georgia (est. 2008; reinitiated 2013), Iraq (est. 2012; reinitiated 2019), Jordan (est. 2020), Kazakhstan (est. 2007), Mauritania (est. 2012), Moldova (est. 2009), Mongolia (est. 2013), Morocco (est. 2019), Serbia (est. 2013), Tunisia (est. 2016), Ukraine (est. 2013), and Uzbekistan (est. 2013). As a NATO DEEP effort, the North Macedonia program concluded in 2020 when the country formally joined NATO in March of that year. Although the NATO program ended, the U.S.-only DEEP has continued with North Macedonia.

FIGURE 2.2

DEEP Events by Year and Funding Source, 2018–2020

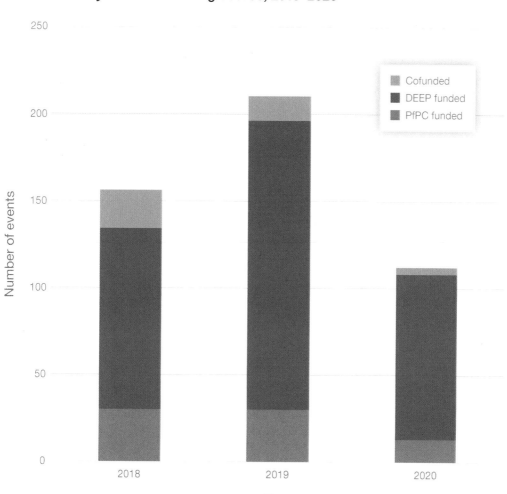

SOURCE: RAND analysis of program event tracking data from NATO, 2020; PfPC, 2020.

data collection and event coding, the data offer a useful illustration of the trend in DEEP activity and, crucially, highlight the cost-sharing structure that underlies the program.

The effects of the pandemic on DEEP can also be seen in Figure 2.3, which plots the number of events per year that were conducted in person or online. In a normal year, program events are conducted across Europe, Africa, Asia, and the United States, hosted by DEEP providers (e.g., a PfPC workshop in Oberammergau, Germany) and beneficiaries (e.g., a NATO SME visit to Yerevan, Armenia) alike. Throughout 2018 and 2019, these events all included an in-person component, which often required international travel by experts, partners, or both. With the onset of the pandemic, however, 54 percent of events in 2020 became virtual, and many were hosted on the newly developed NATO online platform. Using this platform, DEEP

FIGURE 2.3

DEEP Events by Year and Instructional Type, 2018–2020

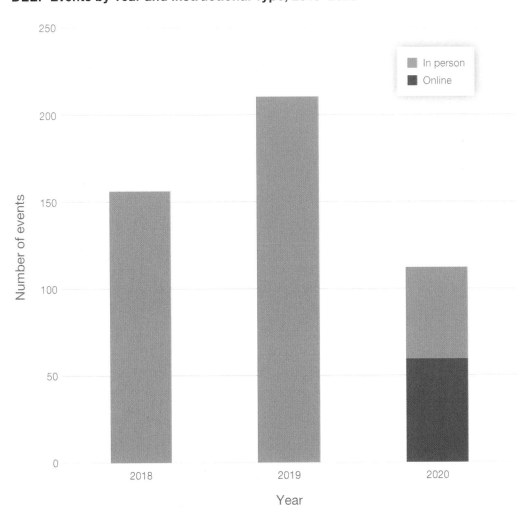

SOURCE: RAND analysis of program event tracking data from NATO, 2020; PfPC, 2020.

officers have not only executed events but also trained partner personnel to use the platform as an academic delivery mechanism (Stolberg, 2020a).

By contrast, there is far more variation in the number of events by country. Even a cursory glance at Figure 2.4 reveals the outlier status of Ukraine, a country program that is vastly larger in size and scope than any other DEEP-supported country. From 2018 through 2020, Ukraine's 242 events accounted for just over one-half of all DEEP events. The next most active program was Tunisia, which had only 41 events during this period. At the other end of the continuum, some country programs, such as Mongolia and Morocco, had only a handful of events.

FIGURE 2.4

DEEP Events by Country, 2018–2020

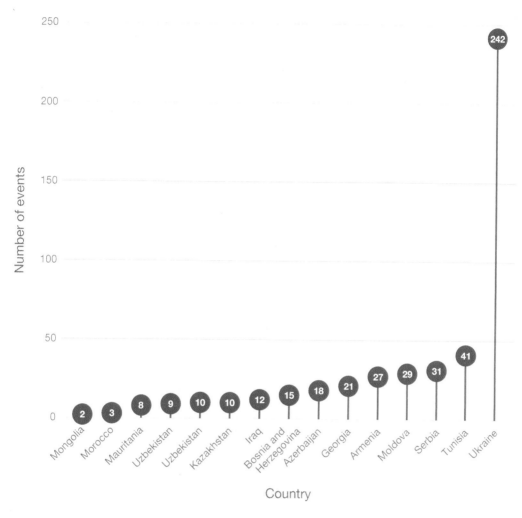

SOURCE: RAND analysis of program event tracking data from NATO, 2020; PfPC, 2020.

Although these differences are stark and should not be discounted, some caveats are required. These aggregate counts might show variation in the number of discrete events and help describe overall activity, but they cannot capture the range or mix of program activities. DEEP efforts include a diverse set of activities, which often vary in length and substantive focus. Thus, for some smaller country programs, the raw count of events might not adequately reflect the overall level of effort or activity.

Conclusion

In this chapter, we provided a brief overview of DEEP efforts between January 2018 and December 2020. During this period, DEEP made several advances in planning and AM&E by incorporating SMART objectives in its annual strategic plans and developing more rigorous measures of effectiveness and monitoring reports.

At the same time, DEEP continued to expand its defense education program to other partner countries and schools while growing the set of curricula and areas of support. We drew on event data to summarize some of these efforts and illustrate the program's growth during this period. These data have also helped us unpack some of the disruptive effects of the COVID-19 pandemic, which has forced the program to adjust its support and rely more heavily on virtual-based instruction.

Although these data can illustrate topline activity levels and broad efforts, they are too coarse to capture country-level program variation and evolution over time. In the next chapter, we explore such variation and describe country program efforts in greater depth through three illustrative cases.

CHAPTER THREE

Program Challenges and Drivers of Success

Having summarized the program's major objectives and efforts from 2018 through 2020, we now dive deeper into our three cases—Armenia, Tunisia, and Ukraine programs. Although each country program faces its own distinct challenges at times, some structural, institutional, and political hurdles are common. Such challenges can be found in various contexts and can significantly impede program efforts. Often, these impediments cannot be fully resolved; program success instead depends on finding mitigation strategies that can effectively defuse tensions, mollify resistance from stakeholders, and create opportunities to work within existing systems while promoting positive change. These case studies highlight some of the major challenges that DEEP country programs often face in planning and executing their efforts over time and illustrate the mitigation strategies that have been employed.

The chapter begins with a brief discussion of our methodological approach and our case selection criteria. We then begin tracing program challenges, evolution, and progress in our three cases. We discuss the problem of stakeholder resistance in Armenia and how persistence ultimately paid off for DEEP efforts. Next, we consider how PME institutional constraints can limit program efforts, as has been the case in Tunisia, where program managers have worked with local partners to tailor efforts to their specific needs. Finally, we turn to the case of Ukraine, which illustrates how DEEP's distinct multinational approach can be critical to making breakthroughs with partner schools and institutions, especially when broader structural and cultural challenges benefit from a diverse mix of DEEP providers. We conclude the chapter with a brief note on generalizability, discussing the degree to which our findings represent other DEEP country programs and can be applied to other ICB efforts.

Methodological Approach and Case Selection

Using a mixed-methods approach, our case studies draw on a variety of data and documents, including planning materials, annual AM&E reports, program activity and event data, AARs, official correspondence, academic studies, think tank reports, and interviews with program stakeholders. Among these various sources, the interviews were particularly important to constructing our case studies, providing insider accounts of how DEEP country programs evolved over time as they confronted challenges along the way. Most of these interviews (six of nine) were with DEEP officers who oversee individual country programs and academic leads who provide subject matter expertise while working with partner officials to shape program design and execution. The remaining three interviews were with NATO and PfPC staff who provide overall program management, which offers a broader perspective than any individual country program. These accounts, however, offer an incomplete picture, omitting essential perspectives—those of partner staff, instructors, students, and other officials.[1]

Using these materials, we employ a process-tracing approach that explores program evolution by focusing on key challenges and inflection points in each of our cases. This approach helps us capture "snapshots at a series of specific moments" of country programs, tracing how efforts evolved in response to different challenges and the underlying drivers of success that helped mitigate these problems (Collier, 2011). We conclude each case study by considering the prospects for future efforts as these programs continue to evolve.

In choosing our cases, we considered several selection criteria, including program age, size, and scope (see Table 3.1). *Program age* is the number of years since the country program's inception. We use December 2020 as the endpoint for this measure. As the table makes clear, our cases vary widely in age, with Armenia the oldest, Tunisia the youngest, and Ukraine falling between the two.

Program size is estimated by the total number of DEEP events executed from 2018 through 2020 for that country program. A raw count of activities is an admittedly coarse measure for program size, especially given the different ways that NATO and the PfPC count events, but it at least provides a rough order of magnitude for total program output. By this measure, the difference between Ukraine—which is by far the largest DEEP country program—and the other cases is significant.

This difference in size is also reflected in *program scope*, which refers to the number of distinct PME institutions at which DEEP operates in a country. These PME institutions include not only war colleges and staff colleges but also NCO academies. As before, the Ukraine country program is significantly broader in scope, reaching 11 distinct institutions, whereas the other country programs touch only a handful of institutions. This issue of scope is nontrivial: In the case of Ukraine, DEEP efforts are conducted at institutions as varied as the war collage– and staff college–level NDU, naval precommissioning academy, and Air Force NCO training center.

In selecting our cases, we tried to strike a balance among these three criteria, but our choice of country programs suffers from some bias, which could limit the results' generalizability. This bias is most pronounced when it comes to program size. Although our sample varies widely in both program age and scope, none of our cases fall on the lower end of program size. Even the smallest program we consider, Armenia, is significantly more active than programs, such as Mauritania's, which has conducted only eight events since 2018. In part, this choice was deliberate and reflects a minimal threshold of activity needed to generate useful insights. Although the sample would be more balanced in size had we selected

---

[1] This study was conducted during the COVID-19 pandemic, which limited the research team's ability to travel and conduct in-person interviews with partner officials.

TABLE 3.1

Case Selection Criteria

DEEP Country Program	Program Age[a]	Program Size[b]	Program Scope[c]
Afghanistan	11 years	10 events	1 institution
Armenia	12 years	27 events	4 institutions
Azerbaijan	11 years	18 events	2 institutions
Bosnia and Herzegovina	2 years	15 events	1 institution
Georgia	8 years[d]	21 events	3 institutions
Iraq	2 years[d]	12 events	3 institutions
Jordan	1 year	0 events (new program)	1 institution
Kazakhstan	14 years	10 events	4 institutions
Mauritania	9 years	8 events	1 institution
Moldova	12 years	29 events	2 institutions
Mongolia	8 years	2 events	1 institution
Morocco	2 years	3 events	2 institutions
North Macedonia	4 years	40 events	2 institutions
Serbia	8 years	31 events	1 institution
Tunisia	5 years	41 events	2 institutions
Ukraine	8 years	242 events	11 institutions
Uzbekistan	8 years	9 events	1 institution

SOURCE: These data draw on official event activity reports from NATO and the PfPC.

[a] Program age represents the time since the country program was initiated.

[b] Program size is the total number of DEEP events from 2018 through 2020.

[c] Program scope refers to the number of distinct PME institutions at which DEEP operates.

[d] The country program was suspended at some point and age represents the number of years since it was reinitiated.

a smaller country program, this balance would come at the expense of sufficient data and documentation to conduct a useful case study.

Armenia: Stakeholder Resistance and Political Change

The importance of stakeholders and their potential resistance to reform have long been a focus in theories of change management and organizational development (Harvey and Broyles, 2010; Le Fevre, 2014; Ortiz, 2012). Such challenges are especially common in educational settings,[2] where resistance to change and innovation is a "perennial phenomenon" among instructors and administrators (Terhart, 2013).

Like any institutional reform program, DEEP critically depends on engaging with and securing the support of local stakeholders. And stakeholder resistance is no less significant when it comes to DEEP. For many partner countries, the list of stakeholders is expansive, from faculty and administrators at a PME institution and senior officers within the general staff to the MOD and its senior civilian leadership. Depending on the specific country and its structures of civilian-military rule, any number of these groups could play an integral role in the development, execution, and success of a DEEP effort. Rarely does increasing the number and diversity of stakeholders make things easier. Instead, the myriad of potential stakeholders, both civilian and military—many of whom may have complicated political and personal interests at stake—often introduces challenges that can lead to obstruction, resistance, and slow progress.

These stakeholder dynamics can be seen in the case of Armenia, where some DEEP efforts were long frustrated by the limited support, if not active resistance, from key stakeholders. The Armenia country program began in 2009, and, since its inception, it has comprised several lines of effort, including an initiative focused on developing a professional NCO school (PfPC, 2020c). Although the overall country program enjoyed some early success on several fronts, there was little progress in terms of NCO development. Over the next decade, DEEP program managers and academic leads continued to stress the importance of NCO development. But as recently as 2018, the DEEP strategic plan for Armenia noted that the country's military education system lacks a "modern and well-established NCO academy" and that "the existing institutions are deficient both in a modern curriculum and the expert instructional staff to teach it" (PfPC, 2016a).

DEEP efforts to develop this NCO academy yielded little progress until spring 2018, when massive political upheaval upended the sitting government, having vast ramifications across Armenian society and the military. On April 17, 2018, the Armenian National Assembly elected Serzh Sargsyan as the new prime minister. Sargsyan had just served as president and, having previously promised not to run for prime minister, his appointment was widely viewed as a corrupt "power grab," which galvanized the opposition and its protest leader, Nikol Pashinian (Gabrielian et al., 2018). After street protests roiled the country and included visible support from the military, Sargsyan resigned less than a week later on April 23, 2018 (Feldman and Alibašić, 2019). With the swift collapse of the Sargsyan government, Pashinian became prime minister on May 8, 2018, ushering in a new political period for the country.

Although similar to other revolutions in post-Soviet states, Armenia's 2018 Velvet Revolution notably differs in several ways, especially when it comes to Russia. In Ukraine and Georgia, for example, domestic political upheaval also disrupted foreign relations with Russia. In Armenia, by contrast, the new prime minister quickly made it clear that the country would

---

[2] For more on resistance in education reform, see Achinstein and Ogawa, 2006; Baum, 2002; and Berkovich, 2011.

honor its international obligations to Russia, "accepting Russian military bases and Russian border guards, as well as maintaining Armenia's membership in Russian-led intergovernmental institutions" (Lanskoy and Suthers, 2019). Notwithstanding this commitment, Pashinian's government has tried to strike a delicate balancing act, maintaining ties with its longtime economic and security partner Russia while also pivoting to "Europe and the West for technical inspiration and material support" (Jennings, 2019). Under Pashinian, Armenia has pursued a variety of political and structural reforms, including efforts targeted at the security sector. In February 2020, these efforts culminated in the inauguration of a "new national multi-stakeholder platform on democratic security sector oversight" intended to increase civilian control over security institutions through an inclusive framework comprising government and civil society organizations (Organization for Security and Co-operation in Europe, 2020).

These political changes have also had a major effect on DEEP efforts, removing obstacles to reform and creating new opportunities for the program. After the 2018 Velvet Revolution, civilian control over the military increased, giving the MOD more influence over training. According to one DEEP officer, these changes could be felt across Armenia's PME institutions, where administrative leaders were replaced with individuals more willing to support educational reforms. The importance of such leadership cannot be overstated and has been seen in other country programs as well, such as Georgia's, where internal leadership changes were reported to have helped streamline and improve management practices at the Georgian National Defense Academy (PfPC EDWG, 2020a). As one DEEP officer explained, "If you really want change, you need leadership that is committed to this change and wants this change and is aware that this change is a threat to someone and that, in turn, someone may try to impede changes."

Finding leaders committed to such change has been especially important to making progress on NCO development. And arguably, nowhere is this new leadership more important than in the general staff. According to one DEEP program manager, there have traditionally been "two worlds" in Armenia, where the "MOD has always been more progressive and leaning towards Western doctrine . . . but in the general staff, all colonels and above were trained in Moscow." Whereas the MOD is responsible for military education (e.g., classroom-based instruction for officers who normally focus on the strategic and operational levels of warfare), the general staff has always controlled the NCO Corps and its training (e.g., usually field-based tactical-oriented instruction on basic soldier skills). The 2018 DEEP Strategic Plan for Armenia attributed limited progress in NCO development to the "apparent lack of attention paid by the Armenian Armed Forces senior leadership to the issue of professional NCO Corps development," and to the "strong conservative bias within the senior ranks that resists change" (PfPC, 2018). Although such attitudes might be slow to change, sudden political upheaval can force the old guard to adapt or face being replaced.

With new leaders empowered, support for NCO development really began to grow in February 2019, when DEEP arranged for the Deputy Chief of Defense to visit the Lithuanian NCO Academy. Drawing on support from Lithuania, DEEP began supporting Armenia's development of a "coherent NCO concept" for its armed forces (PfPC, 2020c). A month later, the MOD issued a decree to develop a professional NCO Corps, and DEEP reports indicate that "senior officers in the general staff have also expressed such interest. This is a substantial step forward, since in the past the senior military leadership did not show significant interest in the development of an NCO Corps" (PfPC, 2020c). Later that year, the Deputy Minister wrote a letter, emphasizing that "we have decided to focus more on the missing link between the soldiers and officers, e.g., the development of a professional Non-Commissioned Officer corps,"[3] and he requested that DEEP support these efforts. In reflecting on this sudden progress after years of resistance, one DEEP program manager concluded that, "Without the change in April 2018, this would not have happened."

But it would be a gross oversimplification to suggest that political upheaval is sufficient on its own to create such change. Underlying all this progress are the years of effort that DEEP program managers, academic leads, and SMEs spent working with Armenians, building relationships, and earning their trust. As one DEEP academic lead put it, "it has taken a long time to break into the general staff side, but we have done it by persisting and trying to help them develop a professional NCO Corps." Institution building is a long game, and it benefits from a continuity of effort with program managers and academic leads who work with the same country for years, "forming a team that goes back, year after year after year" to grow trust and familiarity over time, according to that same individual. Despite resistance among some stakeholders, DEEP efforts persisted in Armenia, slowly building relationships until political changes created new opportunities for the program.

These gains, while encouraging, are fragile. The case of Armenia highlights not only the positive ways that external events can shape program efforts but also the risks. In 2020, DEEP progress in Armenia stalled, first because of the COVID-19 pandemic and then because of war. In September 2020, Armenia clashed with its neighbor Azerbaijan over control of Nagorno-Karabakh, setting off a six-week war that, according to reports from *The New York Times*, left Armenia badly defeated and "deeply reliant on Russia for security, potentially weakening Armenia's independence" (Kramer, 2021). After brokering a ceasefire, Russian peacekeepers deployed to Nagorno-Karabakh, growing Moscow's influence in the country and leading one DEEP officer to lament how the program's gains were at risk "just as we were making progress." According to this officer, some key supporters of DEEP have either been replaced or resigned since the war, and their positions have been filled with more-traditional, Russian-trained officials. Although it is not clear what impact this will have on the program, it reveals the potential fragility of these gains.

---

[3] The Deputy Minister's letter was quoted in Armenia's Strategic Plan for 2020, see PfPC, 2020c.

Tunisia: Institutional Constraints and Demand-Driven Programming

Beyond navigating individual stakeholders and their potential resistance, DEEP efforts must also navigate the challenges of working with local PME institutions, which can vary widely in their organizational structures and missions. At times, these differences could constrain DEEP efforts' scope and ambition. Institutional constraints at a PME college, such as course length, degree requirements, or even the student body, can initially pose challenges for DEEP officers and result in a poor match between program efforts and partner expectations. When local partners perceive a disconnect, it can lead to resistance at the administrative or institutional level, even if senior civilian or military leaders support the program.

Studies of organizational change, whether in firms or schools, suggest that the resistance to reform often revolves around the following three core questions (Terhart, 2013):

- Why change things?
- How will that work?
- What is in it for me?

These questions are just as relevant to DEEP efforts, especially in the early design stages when DEEP officers initially engage with partners and begin identifying priorities and lines of effort. For reform to succeed, these questions need to be addressed in a way that satisfies a local institution's leadership (e.g., commandant), securing their buy-in and support by demonstrating the need, value, and feasibility of program efforts. And as the Tunisia case reveals, DEEP's demand-driven approach to program design could help reassure partners that program efforts will meet their needs.

Of our three case studies, Tunisia is the newest country program. The program began in 2016 after the Tunisian Ministry of National Defense made a written request to explore cooperation opportunities with NATO and the PfPC (PfPC, 2020b). This request came only five years after Tunisia's democratic revolution, which ushered in a new government and major leadership change in the armed forces (Santini and Cimini, 2019). Since the Arab Spring, Tunisia has experienced a rocky transition beset with political and economic instability and terrorism. Given these challenges, security sector reform has become a priority for the nascent democracy's leaders, who have focused their efforts on the internal security forces (e.g., intelligence services and police), which had historically been structured into organizational silos and used to suppress domestic opposition and safeguard the Ben Ali regime (Kartas, 2014). The Tunisian Armed Forces, by contrast, are widely recognized as well trained and highly professional, which they demonstrated in 2011 when they refused to turn their weapons on peaceful protesters (Kartas, 2014). Although broader reforms might be unnecessary for the Tunisian Armed Forces, even these forces, including their PME institutions, need to modernize (PfPC, 2020b), which motivated the launch of DEEP in 2016.

Beginning with the program's initial site visit in March 2016, DEEP activities have concentrated on several lines of effort split across two PME institutions, the war college and the staff college (d'Andurain, 2016). Early efforts focused on curriculum development for new courses taught with a joint perspective (e.g., Operational Art, Planning, and Peacekeeping) and foundational faculty development (PfPC, 2020b). Since its inception, the program has enjoyed some notable successes, including the development of several new courses that are being taught regularly by partner faculty. However, many of these achievements resulted from efforts focused on the war college, even though the staff college has also been a priority since the program began.

According to several DEEP officers, the relative lack of progress at the staff college has been disappointing but somewhat predictable, resulting from institutional features that constrain program support. Based on its organizational structure, existing curriculum, and student body, the war college is simply a more direct fit for a DEEP provider than the staff college. Similar to a Western country's war college, the Tunisian war college's student body comprises "lieutenant colonels and equivalents (NATO OF-4) with an average age of 46 years," most of whom will be "assigned to regiments or higher military HQs" upon graduation (d'Andurain, 2016). The staff college, by contrast, serves a student body comprising more-junior officers: "majors and equivalents (NATO OF-3), with an average age of 41 years," whose future assignments vary widely, from administrative positions to company commanders (d'Andurain, 2016). This difference in student population is important because DEEP efforts typically engage more-senior officers who already have a strong foundation in tactics and are preparing for higher command position.

In addition to these differences in student population, the institutions vary in the types of courses they offer. Whereas the war college's curriculum includes courses on operational planning, combined arms, and command, courses at the staff college tend be at the "higher part of the tactical level and the lower part of the operational level of warfare" (d'Andurain, 2016). Western staff colleges typically teach only at the operational or strategic level of war, and, as such, they are less prepared to engage on more-tactical issues, which could require significant revisions to existing materials or development of new curricula. The courses also vary in their length: War college sessions are twice as long as staff college courses (ten months versus five months, respectively) (d'Andurain, 2016). The result is that Western staff college–equivalent education would normally be split among two or three different schools (e.g., staff college, junior command and staff college, and captain's career course), making the DEEP support effort for the Tunisian staff college somewhat more complex.[4]

These differences, while seemingly minor, have been consequential for DEEP, introducing challenges for program design, especially from the perspective of leadership at the staff college. At the beginning of the program, leaders at the staff college were more skeptical of the value that DEEP could provide, suggesting that the more-tactical level and short duration of

---

[4] For an example of typical Western PME at the tactical, operational, and strategic levels of war, see Solis, 2020.

courses limit the opportunities for incorporating new concepts. For leaders at the Tunisian staff college, their mission is clear: provide basic officer instruction to prepare their students to execute administrative functions and become company commanders. Given their mandate and the time available, leaders initially resisted some of the DEEP offerings, whereas the war college was more open to and supportive of program efforts.

Although initially challenging, DEEP is intended to be demand driven and does not impose any given model or follow a one-size-fits-all approach. DEEP's success depends on program officers working with partners to tailor country programs to partners' and institutions' specific needs, encouraging local ownership to ensure broad stakeholder engagement and support. One longtime DEEP officer described his initial approach with partners as follows:

> I always begin by saying, "I have good news and bad news. The good news: We are not aliens coming to conquer your planet. You are the masters of your destiny. The bad news: You have to work and develop a system that fits your country and your society."

Another program manager described how the DEEP model is fundamentally about dialogue between NATO and its partners, exploring "what kinds of ideas might work, and which ones have been carried out in the past and the challenges they faced." In the case of Georgia, for example, DEEP provided curriculum development events on asymmetric warfare to support the National Defense Academy's new four-year program on defense studies. At the time, the Georgian instructors were not well versed in new concepts of warfare (PfPC EDWG, 2020a).

In terms of effort design, one DEEP academic lead stated that program officers try to work with partners to ensure that activities are shaped by local context and PME institutional needs. This shaping effort is an ongoing process; DEEP officers and academic leads play an essential role as they routinely engage with local stakeholders to identify their needs and communicate those requirements to NATO and PfPC leadership. According to the DEEP academic lead, the annual DEEP Clearing House meeting is critical to this process, giving program officers and partners an opportunity to discuss needs and identify providers who can fill requirements. This matching event allows partners to tailor future efforts, ensuring that activities fit their institutional needs and constraints.

As the support program for the staff college in Tunisia evolved, it became apparent to both the DEEP team and the staff college leadership that DEEP did have capacity to assist with certain tactical-level staff college initiatives not initially considered by either actor at the beginning of the relationship in 2016. This included requests for support for new course curriculum development in tactical-level planning and crisis management in 2019 and tactical-level command, control, communications, information, and leadership in 2020 (Carriero, 2019; NATO International Staff, 2020). Program managers have used these meetings to develop more relevant offerings to the staff college, including new tactical-level courses on contingency planning, integrated communications, and leadership (Carriero, 2020).

Ukraine: Structural Challenges and the Multinational Approach

The most-common challenges to DEEP efforts are the entrenched norms, organizational structures, and historical institutions that block reform.[5] These challenges are not only present in many countries but are often the most difficult to resolve, making ICB a generational endeavor. Such structural challenges in a partner military can be particularly pronounced in former Eastern Bloc states, where a long history of Soviet/Russian military practice limits potential opportunities and requires ICB programs to work around entrenched systems. Although requiring greater coordination, DEEP seeks to overcome these challenges by incorporating a multinational approach that leverages the experiences of multiple providers to find the best fit for partners.

There is an expansive literature exploring the Soviet legacy on political, economic, social and cultural institutions in former Soviet states.[6] These legacy effects are often no less pronounced in the military domain, where "the management essence of the Soviet and then Russian culture was in highly centralized command-like decision making" (Bugriy, 2018). These top-down Soviet command and control structures have systemic implications, shaping incentives and organizational choices throughout the military. For many of these states, the long history of Soviet rule continues to have an enduring effect on their military structures, training, and practices, which often conflict with Western models, creating major obstacles to interoperability and joint warfighting (Oliker et al., 2016). Reform efforts in Ukraine not only illustrate many of these challenges but also reveal how DEEP is designed to overcome such obstacles.

The Ukraine program began in 2013 and has since grown to be the largest DEEP country program. This growth is all the more impressive (and needed) given the many structural challenges that Ukraine faces as it modernizes its armed forces. These challenges go back to the very beginning of the post-Soviet period. In the mid-1990s, then-president Leonid Kuchma "instructed his military officers to look to both Cossack and Soviet traditions to help them in the construction of new Ukrainian armed forces" (Kuzio, 1998). But the Soviet influence is more than just modeling. With the sudden dissolution of the Soviet Union, more than 700,000 Soviet soldiers were left in Ukraine, and the newly independent government decided to the nationalize these forces (Perepelitsa, 2002). These choices "affected both force structure and military culture" and have had an enduring effect on Ukraine's military (Perepelitsa, 2002). Authors of a 2016 RAND report found that, "While there have been major improvements on the Soviet-era institutions that Ukraine initially inherited, Ukraine's cur-

---

[5] In addition to the country case studies, our analysis also drew on a broader review of program AM&E materials, which described planning and execution challenges across the DEEP portfolio. This comparative analysis is the focus of Chapter Four and draws heavily on annual monitoring and evaluation reports; see PfPC EDWG, 2020a.

[6] For a review of this literature, see Laitin, 2000.

rent institutions still reflect a hybrid between those and approaches that reflect Western governance models" (Oliker et al., 2016).

The effects of these Soviet-era institutions can be readily seen across the armed forces and have complicated DEEP efforts in myriad ways. At a strategic level, Ukraine's military was "structured around Soviet threat assessments and doctrines," which has shaped its approach to military education, training, and decisionmaking processes (Bugriy, 2018; Perepelitsa, 2002; PfPC EDWG, 2020a). The Ukrainian Armed Forces' (UAF's) logistics system is also "a carryover from the Soviet Union and does not follow the structure of logistics systems in NATO countries" (Oliker et al., 2016). Even organizational structures as basic as tactical units depart from NATO standards; companies in NATO militaries comprise four platoons, whereas Ukrainian companies are "three-unit" based (Bugriy, 2018). These Soviet-era standards and practices not only hinder "warfighting effectiveness, internal interoperability, and relationships with NATO suppliers and partners" but also complicate DEEP efforts and require program officers to work in the existing structures as they gradually change over time (Oliker et al., 2016).

This need for programmatic patience and flexibility is especially important because these Soviet structures are slow to change and are often integral to how these militaries function. And although Soviet-modeled systems might be inefficient, "simply changing the structure to NATO standards may result initially in decreased performance of the military" (Bugriy, 2018). For countries like Ukraine, such performance costs could be prohibitively high. As one DEEP officer noted, "You can't change systems while in a fight." Given this constraint, program officers must be careful where and how they push reform: "Introducing new training for NATO standards can be a waste of time unless you change other structures." And even if an effort meets its specific objectives, the benefits might be limited if the partner cannot sustain the investment. These risks are a constant concern for program officers working in Ukraine, who have to plan around structures that might not support, encourage, or reward officers who develop new skills or knowledge. We spoke with one academic expert who described how Ukrainian officers are not sufficiently incentivized to acquire new skills and often do not get an opportunity to use them in their positions, leading to erosion of these skills over time.

These structural challenges might be complicated, but DEEP's distinct multinational approach provides a means to better navigate, if not always overcome, such barriers to reform. For every DEEP country program, multinational teams of experts serve as the providers of curriculum and faculty development, leveraging their diverse expertise, skills, and experiences, offering partner schools a wide choice of provider (NATO International Staff, 2019b). According to a DEEP official, this multinational team will often consist of a majority of specialists from one country (e.g., the United States or Canada), but those specialists will work with other providers who have a better understanding of the partner nation and can assist by drawing on shared experiences, language, and history.

In the case of Ukraine, DEEP efforts have drawn heavily on providers who have experience transitioning from the legacy of Soviet military systems and practices, including those from Poland and the Baltic states.[7] Among these providers, Lithuania has been especially important, drawing on its experience to support DEEP efforts on topics as varied as NCO development and training for military police and special operations forces. The Lithuanian NCO school has similarly supported Moldova's efforts to develop a comprehensive NCO program (PfPC EDWG, 2020a). Compared with Ukraine, Lithuania inherited relatively less from Soviet rule, having largely created its armed forces anew in 1990 (Urbelis and Urbonas, 2002). Drawing on volunteers and former Soviet officers, "the new structure and doctrine of the Lithuanian military reflect a more Western approach to military reform," although residual Soviet influence initially led to some "resistance to the westernization of Lithuanian military norms and values" (Urbelis and Urbonas, 2002). Several DEEP program managers described how this shared cultural experience was especially important early in the Ukraine program, helping Ukrainians to become more comfortable with DEEP and to buy into its efforts.

In addition to cultural and historical experiences, there are also substantive differences in DEEP providers' missions, organizations, and resources, which make some providers a better fit than others for a given partner. The curricula in the Baltic Defence College, for example, adhere to NATO standards but vary from those used in the U.S. command and general staff college or U.S. Army War College.[8] These differences can often be important, making some models more useful than others for a country program or partner to replicate. A Lithuanian officer involved in the Ukraine country program described how

> [s]ome NATO countries have been building their systems slowly for 100 years, but we know what it takes [to transition from Soviet rule]. Our experience is useful for Ukraine, and they accept that. The U.S. model may be the best in the world, but it's impossible to make it workable in Ukraine. Still, Ukraine can't copy Lithuania because it is much bigger and changes will require more work and time, but they can learn things from our experience.

DEEP's multinational approach offers other benefits as well, particularly when it comes to burden sharing. All providers, however well resourced and capable they might be, face their own constraints. And in some cases, a given provider might not be able to offer sufficient expertise on a particular topic. According to one DEEP official, having a deep bench of multinational providers expands the range of possible topics that a DEEP country program can cover by leveraging multiple partners. In other cases, the scope of a given program's

---

[7] Initially, Poland was critical, but after 2015, NATO members became more sensitive to providing some forms of support that could further escalate tensions with Russia. Lithuania was willing to provide more support under these tense conditions. This background derives from an author interview with a DEEP official.

[8] U.S. PME institutions and their curricula are designed around global mission sets and can assume commanders will have access to sophisticated weapons systems, intelligence, surveillance, and reconnaissance, and expansive logistics networks to sustain their forces. However, many partners do not enjoy ready access to such assets and resources, and their missions tend to be more limited and focused on territorial defense. On these dimensions alone, the Baltic Defence College makes for a much cleaner match for Ukraine's NDU.

effort might be overwhelming, making the shared approach not just preferred but necessary. According to a NATO official, for countries like Ukraine—where DEEP efforts span 11 PME institutions that include the UAF's ground, naval, and air forces and serve military officers, NCOs, and civilians—no single provider "can afford to build these institutions on their own." With activities spread across so many institutions, these efforts "do not benefit from economies of scale, experiences from one institution (or service) cannot be passed on to the others seamlessly, and effort is thinned out across the territory" (Jolicoeur, 2018).

Summary Insights

In this chapter, we explored three illustrative cases—Armenia, Tunisia, and Ukraine—that reveal some of the major challenges that DEEP efforts often face and how they are designed to overcome these challenges. In this final section, we discuss the extent and conditions under which these cases' lessons generalize more broadly, both in the DEEP portfolio and beyond to other PME or ICB efforts.

In the case of Armenia, we described how complicated personal and professional interests among individual stakeholders in the general staff can lead to resistance, requiring patience and persistence. Such resistance is common in ICB programs and can be particularly pronounced in transitional states in which reform efforts become viewed through a generational lens, creating fear among the old guard that leads to intergenerational conflict. DEEP program managers and academic leads have seen similar challenges in Kazakhstan and Ukraine, where ICB efforts can be seen as a potential threat to the existing order and structure in the armed forces. What distinguishes Armenia from these other cases, however, is the political change in 2018, which empowered new voices in the armed forces and created an opportunity for program efforts to expand. Ultimately, the case reveals how persistence might be a necessary condition, but it is not sufficient for success.

Tunisia's brief history with DEEP, although positive overall, also included some resistance, but this challenge came at the local PME institution level. In contexts like Tunisia, where institutions are already well established and relatively mature, program managers must navigate local PME institutional constraints. Rarely do ICB programs have the luxury of starting anew, unconstrained by existing institutions. Instead, these programs have to work with existing institutions, helping encourage long-term reform while also serving the more immediate needs of the faculty and student body. Although staff college leadership concerns about program fit and relevance initially slowed progress at the staff college, DEEP officers and academic leads worked with local partners to develop a series of efforts tailored to the institution's specific needs. This approach has paid off in other DEEP efforts as well, such as in the Kazakhstan NDU, where more-senior faculty were initially reluctant to accept faculty development support. According to an interview with a NATO DEEP faculty development group in October 2021, the faculty's view changed from 2008 to 2010 after they had a positive experience with the DEEP expert faculty development workshops.

In our final case, we explored how Ukraine's Soviet legacy created deep structural challenges to ICB and PME efforts. Institutional structures are imbued with the history and culture of their founding, likely making them slow to change. These challenges are not only difficult to resolve, often requiring decades of effort, but they are also found in many countries, including those in the DEEP portfolio (e.g., Armenia, Azerbaijan, Georgia, Kazakhstan, and Uzbekistan). DEEP's multinational approach offers a potential advantage in mitigating these challenges by leveraging the diverse experiences of different providers to help countries find the right model and partner with whom they feel most comfortable. Although such an inclusive, multinational approach often requires greater coordination, it could enhance other types of ICB programs in contexts where cultural-historical legacies create structural obstacles to reform.

CHAPTER FOUR

Lessons Learned and Best Practices

In this chapter, we expand our analysis beyond our three case studies by discussing some of the broader lessons learned from the past three years. Through these lessons, we identify potential best practices to support future program growth, focusing on distance-based learning and program AM&E. We begin with the impact of the COVID-19 pandemic, which has disrupted years of planning and forced program managers, academic leads, and SMEs to quickly adapt to new virtual platforms. This disruption has spurred innovation, leading to a dramatic expansion in distance-learning capability, which offers notable efficiency gains. We then describe some of the ongoing challenges related to data collection and the implications for effective AM&E. We highlight alternative strategies for capturing these data, which could help program managers better evaluate DEEP efforts and improve overall program design in the future.

From Disruption to Innovation: Increasing Efficiency Through Distance Learning

Like other PME and ICB programs, DEEP has traditionally relied on in-person engagements and involved considerable international travel. However, with the onset of the COVID-19 pandemic, many of these efforts had to be suspended, and the in-person events were replaced with remote DEEP support through virtual platforms. These platforms entailed a steep learning curve for both providers and partners—introducing both technological and pedagogical challenges—but they have been critical to sustaining program efforts and have introduced significant efficiency gains.

By March 2020, DEEP had already canceled or postponed all previously scheduled program events (NATO DEEP, 2020a). Despite its focus on in-person instruction, the program proved to be especially agile in the early days of the pandemic. Program managers immediately began assessing their options for utilizing virtual platforms and rescheduling events. Compared with many other ICB programs, DEEP enjoyed one major advantage: Distance-based learning programs had already been explored and introduced into the DEEP portfolio of activities. Five years earlier, DEEP developed an Advanced Distributive Learning (ADL)/ Distance Learning Portal to "provide information to partners on how to develop on-line distance learning and provide on-line courses that can be adapted for a distance learning program" (NATO DEEP, 2020b). Although the system was already in place, one program manager noted that the ADL platform "was not heavily used or taken very seriously" before the pandemic. However, once it became clear that program efforts would have to operate virtually for the foreseeable future, DEEP began developing additional support, including a new Distance Learning Reference Curriculum (NATO DEEP, 2020b).

Although this platform and support for it has had to evolve over time to meet increasing demand, technology was not the biggest challenge facing DEEP and its partners. The shift to virtual platforms forced schools to develop and refine their pedagogy for distance learning or *blended learning* (a combination of resident and nonresident instruction). These changes disrupted the traditional way that many providers and partners had operated. One program manager described how the human factor was especially challenging, as many instructors were never previously trained in how to conduct courses online. For some partners, there is a distrust or other sensitivities around using a virtual platform, which might not always be secure.

According to one NATO official, DEEP officers, academic leads, and partners all became more comfortable using virtual platforms over time. These practices have become increasingly routine as more events are conducted virtually. By March 2020, Moldova's ADL program consisted of over 20 courses and more than 2,000 users (PfPC EDWG, 2020a). With this new technology and support framework in place, DEEP has used virtual engagements to replace, albeit imperfectly, a wide range of in-person activities and events. These engagements include initial site surveys and scoping visits for Iraq and Jordan;[1] annual country program reviews;[2] faculty development workshops;[3] curriculum development workshops;[4] and even large conference meetings, such as the PfPC EDWG and the annual DEEP Clearing House, which included 99 participants over seven days in September 2020.[5] Crucially, the platform has also been used to host workshops on the best practices and lessons learned for the trans-

---

[1] New site survey and scoping visits were executed virtually (e.g., Iraq Ministerial Training Defence College and Jordan NCO Training Center previsits). They took place several hours per day over one or two days. The first of a two-part initial site survey and scoping visit for the Iraq Ministerial Training Defence College took place virtually on November 30, 2020. A preinitial site survey coordination virtual meeting took place with the Jordanian NCO Training Center on October 20, 2020. The only portion of an in-person visit that could not take place was the ability to walk through the training facilities (e.g., classrooms, library, and IT facilities). This portion of a site survey is required to determine if the partner school classrooms are organized in a modern teaching fashion and have all needed resources required for instruction.

[2] They took place three to four hours per day over several days (one to ten working days, depending on the size of the country program).

[3] Examples include October and November 2020 meetings for the Afghanistan MIP Workshop and December 2020 meetings for the Tunisia Basic Faculty Development Workshop.

[4] The subjects of the workshops have included leadership and NCO education and overall curriculum reviews for a school or schools.

[5] The annual EDWG meeting for all country academic leads and program managers was conducted over three hours in one day. For more on the virtual DEEP Clearing House, see NATO Newsroom, 2020a.

formation from resident to distance learning for DEEP providers and partner schools.[6] The November 2020 workshop included 209 participants from across 111 PME institutions who discussed challenges with adapting to distance learning and "exchanged views about training and technology required to make distance-learning courses more effective" (NATO Newsroom, 2020b).

Admittedly, some events are better suited to the virtual approach than others. For example, some DEEP providers found that it was often harder to virtually conduct faculty development workshops because of the emphasis on active learning and the need to include multiple student exercises (NATO DEEP, 2020c). However, the virtual platform has allowed these programs to continue without in-person visits while saving time and money spent on travel. Although initially disruptive, the pandemic has ultimately inspired academic innovation and resulted in greater programmatic agility, cost savings, and efficiency gains that can be sustained long after the pandemic-related travel restrictions end.

The Problem of Data: Improving Effectiveness Through Better AM&E

Recent advances in program planning, including the incorporation of SMART objectives, have improved program design and execution, but major data challenges remain. Evaluating the impact of and learning from a DEEP strategy's past efforts can be difficult due to the lack of student tracking or observation in the postgraduation field. We spoke with one academic lead who described what can (and cannot) be observed, suggesting that longer-term impact must be inferred:

> We don't have evidence on students in the future. If the courses or our support have been effective, we don't really know because we are not in the field. What we do see is an improvement in the way students are educated. . . . Even if we can't see it in the field, we think that they have a greater capability.

DEEP officers simply do not have the means or access to directly contact or readily observe PME graduates after they have completed a DEEP-related course. In some cases, only the former student can fully appreciate the impact of the supported school's curricula and teaching approaches on their career and operational value. This feedback and observation could provide critical information to evaluate past efforts' effectiveness and relevance. Partner support, both at the PME institution and in the military more broadly, will be crucial to overcoming these challenges. Such support is especially important when it comes to collecting longer-term impact and outcome data at the operational level.

---

[6] The Distance Learning Best Practices/Lessons Learned Workshop was conducted virtually on November 16–18, 2020.

The newly developed SMART objectives are useful from a planning perspective and should also shape future data collection efforts. These objectives can serve as a guide to develop clear indicators for performance monitoring and evaluation plans. SMART objectives provide greater fidelity for event goals, delineate timelines to achieve effects, and identify specific conditions for determining program success or failure. Such details are crucial to developing good indicators. For concreteness, consider the following SMART objective from Ukraine's 2020 Strategic Plan (PfPC, 2020g):

- **Specific:** Employ curriculum development to support the collaborative creation of a modern NATO-standard operational and strategic graduate-level logistics course that Ukrainian instructors will deliver without external support.
- **Measurable:** Ukraine NDU faculty are delivering the new NATO-standard graduate-level logistics curriculum without external support within 12–18 months.
- **Achievable:** Ukraine school leadership and faculty are able to support implementation; funding and providers are available.
- **Relevant:** Support logistics self-sufficiency and NATO standardization for the UAF, which are key for interoperability and armed forces professionalization.
- **Time bound:** Pilot course is to be conducted by Ukraine logistics instructors without external support within 12–18 months.

This objective has clear implications for performance monitoring and indicator design. A possible program execution and monitoring plan for this effort could be as follows:

- In the first six to nine months, program officers conduct two or three curriculum development workshops to review existing syllabi, consider NDU requirements, and collaboratively draft written course materials with NDU faculty experts.
- Within nine months of effort initiation, DEEP and partner staff complete the draft curriculum for a graduate-level logistics course.
- In the final six to nine months, program officers convene two or three faculty training and development workshops to train the partner faculty to deliver the new curriculum and revise it as needed.
- Between 18 and 24 months of effort initiation, DEEP officers observe NDU faculty deliver the graduate-level logistics course using the newly drafted curriculum.

In addition to monitoring plans, SMART objectives can also help develop more-rigorous evaluations and better refine outcome measures. With the NDU logistics course, for example, a near-term outcome measure might be the extent to which the new curriculum follows NATO standards on logistics (e.g., NATO classes of supply, modern defense management systems, and standard procedures for sustainment planning). This outcome can be directly evaluated upon completion of the DEEP effort. A longer-term outcome of interest, perhaps a year or two years after completing the curriculum, might be whether NDU faculty have been able to sustain and deliver the course without external support. Program officers can readily observe this outcome measure through follow-up visits or even a desk review of the NDU academic calendar and course listing.

These measures, while useful indicators of whether a program effort has achieved its immediate intent, are insufficient when it comes to broader, long-term impact (e.g., increased partner logistics capacity and greater interoperability with NATO forces). To capture long-term impact, DEEP could develop alumni surveys for partner school graduates. A longitudinal study could explore the value of DEEP-supported education over time as the student's career progresses. With the support of the PME institution, general staff, and/or MOD, a simple and short survey instrument could be distributed by email and used to help identify specific areas in which DEEP efforts (e.g., topics covered in a curriculum and critical thinking skills developed through modern teaching methods) have been relevant and support the former student's professional tasks or responsibilities. Another potential way to more efficiently capture these perspectives would be to engage with graduates of partner PME institutions who are assigned to their country's NATO delegation or to NATO International Military Staff. With many of these officers assigned to Brussels, an AM&E study team could quickly conduct a series of structured interviews on how PME courses enabled them in their assignments at NATO.

Although there is no way to fully eliminate individual student bias, it is often the former student who is best situated to evaluate whether their learning has supported their postgraduation professional duties. Program officers might also consider how observational measures could complement this survey instrument by evaluating whether specific units or even services that have a larger number of former DEEP-affiliated students become more capable and interoperable with NATO over time. An alternative option would be to review the Partnership Action Plans that partner nations submit to NATO. A study team could review these plans over time to evaluate the degree of change in how partner countries are absorbing the impact of critical thinking, the importance of civilian control of the military, and other program objectives. Given the many confounding variables and myriad data limitations, such observational indicators cannot establish a causal relationship but could provide additional suggestive evidence of DEEP's potential impact. Over time, such data can feed back into the planning process, supporting iterative efforts to improve program design and execution.

Summary Insights

In this chapter, we explored some of the broader challenges that DEEP has faced over the past three years and the lessons learned during this time. Like many ICB programs, DEEP has traditionally focused on in-person engagements, many of which have been hosted by partner PME schools. With the COVID-19 pandemic, program managers and officers have had to navigate unprecedented challenges to planning and executing program activities.

Such disruption has spurred innovation. After some initial challenges, most program activities and events transitioned to a virtual platform, giving providers the ability to connect with partners and sustain efforts throughout the pandemic. This platform ensures communication and continuity during periods of restricted travel, but the lack of direct, in-person contact makes this an imperfect substitute. In-person engagement is often critical to building relationships, growing trust, and increasing access in a partner country. These objectives might not be the focus of such engagements, but they can prove to be critical to reforming institutions.

Over the past three years, DEEP officers have also worked to incorporate SMART objectives into strategic plans while developing more-rigorous monitoring and evaluation frameworks. These efforts are promising, but program AM&E continues to suffer from a lack of data, especially measures for key outcomes, such as students' postgraduation career performance. Expanding data collection is critical to rigorous AM&E and can help further improve program planning and execution.

CHAPTER FIVE

Conclusion

In this final chapter, we conclude by summarizing the major challenges that have shaped DEEP in recent years and highlight how the program's core features have helped resolve these obstacles. As seen in the three case studies, DEEP has continued to evolve and mature while navigating the many challenges of operating during a pandemic. We begin by discussing how partner interests and institutional constraints can slow progress. Overcoming these obstacles requires program continuity and consistency; over time, collaboration builds trust, familiarity, and relationships that are key to better understanding (and working around) partners' interests and constraints. We then discuss the challenge of working with so many different partner militaries that have diverse needs and requirements. DEEP's multinational approach helps share this burden while leveraging the expertise of different providers to better meet partner needs. Finally, we conclude with a broader discussion on institutional change and the time it takes to see results. Facing such slow-to-change structures, we make the case for patience and sustained support to help increase returns on investment.

Partner Interests and Institutional Constraints: Building Trust Through Collaboration

Even during normal times, DEEP efforts often depend on program officers' consistency and persistence in working with partners. Continuity helps build trust and relationships that could be critical to navigating thorny politics and local institutions. The shift to distance-based learning and virtual platforms has only made such consistency more important as providers leverage these relationships to remotely sustain program efforts during the pandemic.

Partners' interests and institutions can slow or constrain DEEP progress for an individual school (e.g., Tunisian staff college) or even a whole military (e.g., Armenia). Overcoming these obstacles often depends on persuading partner nation MOD, general staff, and PME school leadership to support DEEP. DEEP efforts have typically been most effective in overcoming stakeholder resistance when there is programmatic consistency and continuity of the DEEP personnel planning and executing the support events. Academic leads and program managers will typically work for years with the same country and partner school leaders and faculty. This kind of sustained engagement can help grow trust and familiarity and build enduring relationships over time.

Such trust is key when it comes to collaborating with partners. Institutional PME school constraints, such as school-mandated course length, specific degree requirements, or a mismatch between when the school needs a new course and the DEEP course development timeline, can result in a poor match between DEEP efforts and the needs of the partner institution. This mismatch introduces DEEP design challenges. When partner PME institution leaders present resistance, DEEP officers work with partner schools to tailor efforts to their specific needs and to encourage local ownership of desired change. This collaborative process works only if partners and providers trust each other and can work together. Such relationships are built through programmatic consistency and continuity.

Diverse Needs and Requirements: Flexibility and Resilience Through a Multinational Approach

During the COVID-19 pandemic, many providers have been limited in their capacity to travel, but DEEP's commitment to a multinational approach has ensured that some in-person efforts have continued despite disruption. DEEP was designed as a collaborative effort between NATO and the PfPC, specifically intended to orchestrate multinational support for the defense education component of ICB. By not relying on a single country to provide support, DEEP can be more resilient in the face of disruption and other challenges.

More than just a source of resilience, this approach provides maximum flexibility to link partners with a more diverse range of providers than would be associated with a bilateral security cooperation effort. Partner countries can be paired with providers with whom they might be more comfortable because of a shared language, culture, or history.[1] And in some cases, partner countries might not be comfortable trying to emulate the U.S. model, which tends to be more global in orientation, more ambitious in mission set, and designed around more-advanced capabilities and greater resources. Given these differences, some partner countries might prefer working with other providers who have faced similar constraints or challenges in transforming their militaries. To help satisfy these needs, curriculum development often leverages academic expertise from across NATO-allied provider schools, many of which have developed their own military doctrine, tactics, and procedures around more-limited missions, objectives, and resources.

The value of this approach has been particularly evident in the case of Ukraine, where providers that were part of the former Soviet Union or the Eastern European component of the Warsaw Pact have played an indispensable role. Those provider nations and their PME systems experienced many of the same trials 20–25 years ago that current NATO partner states are experiencing today as they modernize their education systems. Major structural challenges, like a long history of Soviet/Russian military practice, can constrain potential

---

[1]   The importance of a shared language should not be overlooked. DEEP providers often have to navigate language barriers, especially when partners have limited familiarity with the English language.

opportunities for change and require DEEP efforts to work around entrenched systems as these partner militaries undergo transition. Under such conditions, it helps to have a provider that has personal experience navigating such a transition in their own military.

Admittedly, this collaborative effort can come at a cost, requiring more time and effort for program officers to identify providers, secure resources, and coordinate efforts among multiple countries. And even if a program officer can identify experts for a given topic or area, there is no guarantee that the provider has the capacity or interest to support the program, potentially leaving some needs unmet.

Hard and Slow to Change: Increasing Returns on Investment Through Strategic Patience

Under the best of conditions, ICB efforts often take years to achieve effects, and, as the Armenia case reveals, such efforts might ultimately depend on broader political or structural changes to create openings. These changes can come suddenly and without warning, making it difficult for program managers and academic leads to predict, let alone plan, their activities or resources around such opportunities. But one thing is clear: Seizing these opportunities requires presence and patience.

However, DEEP efforts are relatively inexpensive (e.g., SMEs volunteer their time). The continued utilization of virtual platforms for program support will further reduce DEEP's operational costs. Long-term substantive change of significance in the Euro-Atlantic community will likely continue to increase over time with the expansion of curriculum development support that is formulated and delivered to NATO standards and with the development of faculty who engender critical thinking skills. Curriculum development support is particularly important for subjects that DEEP has continually emphasized, such as integrity building, counterterrorism, leadership and ethics, logistics, officer or NCO relations, and operational and joint planning. The value of faculty development is best seen in students' growing critical thinking skills, which helps security professionals to approach a problem in a similar manner: Question assumptions rather than accept judgment, take calculated risks as opposed to avoiding risk, and anticipate and be proactive instead of being responsive and reactive (Keagle, 2012). These skills have value far beyond the classroom.

But these efforts take time. Like other forms of ICB, DEEP efforts can be thought of as an investment, committing time and resources to build capacity in a PME institution, which then shapes the educational outcomes for future students. The effects of such efforts and the returns on U.S. and NATO investments could take time to mature, requiring patience. However, U.S. and NATO stakeholders cannot be infinitely patient. Program managers have to be strategically patient, identifying conditions that make continuity and persistence a calculated but worthwhile risk. For example, the lack of progress in the Armenia case could at times be attributed to resistance from some stakeholders in the general staff. Although these challenges were notable, they were not insurmountable, especially with growing support from leaders in Armenia's MOD. By maintaining a continuous presence and cultivating relationships, DEEP was well positioned to translate this support into progress on key issues, leading to a breakthrough when political changes provided new windows of opportunity.

Conclusion

DEEP efforts, like most ICB programs, face myriad challenges. Program officers must navigate the thorny politics of partner countries while working to meet the diverse needs of government officials, military leadership, PME staff, instructors, and students. Often, various stakeholders have opposing or conflicting interests, which creates local resistance and obstacles to reform. Given such challenges, PME institutions are slow to change, requiring that DEEP officers remain patient and flexible over time. But even this does not guarantee success. As the Armenia case has shown, gains can be fragile, and the windows of opportunity can be short.

Despite these difficulties, ICB efforts like DEEP could be more important and urgent today than ever before. As the Biden administration continues its strategic shift to the Indo-Pacific region, traditional allies and regional security partners will be asked to shoulder more of the burden to support stability and extended deterrence. Whether confronting a revanchist Russia in Eastern Europe or combating transnational terrorist groups in North Africa, many DEEP partner countries are on the front lines facing these new security threats. More-capable, professional militaries that can interoperate with U.S. and NATO forces could be critical to these efforts and their success.

Abbreviations

AAR	after-action report
ADL	Advanced Distributive Learning
AM&E	assessment, monitoring, and evaluation
COVID-19	coronavirus disease 2019
DCB	Defense and Related Security Capacity Building
DEEP	Defense Education Enhancement Program
DoD	U.S. Department of Defense
EDWG	Education Development Working Group
HSP	human subject protections
ICB	institutional capacity building
MIP	Master Instructor Program
MOD	Ministry of Defense
NATO	North Atlantic Treaty Organization
NCO	noncommissioned officer
NDU	National Defense University
OSD	Office of the Secretary of Defense
PfPC	Partnership for Peace Consortium
PME	professional military education
SMART	specific, measurable, achievable, relevant, and time bound
SME	subject matter expert
UAF	Ukrainian Armed Forces
VSMU	V. Sargsyan Military University
ZMIT	Zhytomyr Military Institute of Technology

References

Achinstein, Betty, and Rodney T. Ogawa, "(In)Fidelity: What the Resistance of New Teachers Reveals About Professional Principles and Prescriptive Policies," *Harvard Educational Review*, Vol. 76, No. 1, 2006, pp. 30–63.

Baum, Howell S., "Why School Systems Resist Reform: A Psychoanalytic Perspective," *Human Relations*, Vol. 55, No. 2, 2002, pp. 173–198.

Berkovich, Izhak, "No, We Won't! Teachers' Resistance to Educational Reform," *Journal of Educational Administration*, Vol. 49, No. 5, 2011, pp. 563–578.

Bugriy, Maksym, "Ukraine's Security Sector Reform: Is Ukraine Taking Western Advice?" *Connections: The Quarterly Journal*, Vol. 17, No. 3, 2018, pp. 72–91.

Carriero, Gianluca, *Defence Education Clearing House DEEP Update for Tunisia*, unpublished briefing, June 18–19, 2019.

Carriero, Gianluca, *Defence Education Enhancement Programme (DEEP) Update for Tunisia (TN)*, briefing, Annual DEEP Clearing House, September 18, 2020.

Collier, David, "Understanding Process Tracing," *PS: Political Science and Politics*, Vol. 44, No. 4, October 2011, pp. 823–830.

d'Andurain, Jean, *Report of the Initial Site Survey for the Tunisia (TN) War College and Staff College*, unpublished, March 2016.

Feldman, Daniel L., and Haris Alibašić, "The Remarkable 2018 'Velvet Revolution': Armenia's Experiment Against Government Corruption," *Public Integrity*, Vol. 21, No. 4, 2019, pp. 420–432.

Gabrielian, Sisak, Karlen Aslanian, Narine Ghalechian, and Amos Chapple, "Lawmakers Approve Sarkisian as Armenia's PM Despite Countrywide Protests," *RadioFreeEurope/ RadioLiberty*, April 17, 2018. As of April 1, 2021:
https://www.rferl.org/a/armenia-opposition-protests-parliament-vote-sarkisian-prime-minister/29172095.html

Harvey, Thomas R., and Elizabeth A. Broyles, *Resistance to Change: A Guide to Harnessing Its Positive Power*, New York: Rowman & Littlefield, 2010.

Heick, Terry, "Bloom's Taxonomy Is a Hierarchical Framework for Cognition and Learning Objectives," TeachThought webpage, updated May 1, 2020. As of December 24, 2020:
https://www.teachthought.com/learning/what-is-blooms-taxonomy-a-definition-for-teachers/

Jennings, Ray Salvatore, "Upgrading U.S. Support for Armenia's Postrevolution Reforms," Carnegie Endowment for International Peace, February 14, 2019.

Jolicoeur, Pierre, "Defense Education Enhancement Program in Ukraine: The Limits of NATO's Education Program," *Connections: The Quarterly Journal*, Vol. 17, No. 3, 2018, pp. 109–119.

Kartas, Moncef, "Foreign Aid and Security Sector Reform in Tunisia: Resistance and Autonomy of the Security Forces," *Mediterranean Politics*, Vol. 19, No. 3, 2014, pp. 373–391.

Keagle, James M., "A Special Relationship: U.S. and NATO Engagement with the Partnership for Peace to Build Partner Capacity Through Education," *Connections*, Vol. 11, No. 4, 2012, pp. 59–74.

Kramer, Andrew E., "Armenia and Azerbaijan: What Sparked War and Will Peace Prevail?" *New York Times*, January 29, 2021.

Kuzio, Taras, "Ukraine: Coming to Terms with the Soviet Legacy," *Journal of Communist Studies and Transition Politics*, Vol. 14, No. 4, 1998, pp. 1–27.

Laitin, David D., "Post-Soviet Politics," *Annual Review of Political Science*, Vol. 3, 2000, pp. 117–148.

Lanskoy, Miriam, and Elspeth Suthers, "Armenia's Velvet Revolution," *Journal of Democracy*, Vol. 30, No. 2, 2019, pp. 85–99.

Le Fevre, Deidre M., "Barriers to Implementing Pedagogical Change: The Role of Teachers' Perceptions of Risk," *Teaching and Teacher Education*, Vol. 38, February 2014, pp. 56–64.

Magalotti, Daniel, "U.S. National Defense University, Ukraine (NDU) Visit Draft Agenda," Draft schedule, February 17, 2016.

Marquis, Jefferson P., Michael J. McNerney, S. Rebecca Zimmerman, Merrie Archer, Jeremy Boback, and David Stebbins, *Developing an Assessment, Monitoring, and Evaluation Framework for U.S. Department of Defense Security Cooperation*, Santa Monica, Calif.: RAND Corporation, RR-1611-OSD, 2016. As of May 4, 2022: https://www.rand.org/pubs/research_reports/RR1611.html

McNerney, Michael J., Jefferson P. Marquis, S. Rebecca Zimmerman, and Ariel Klein, *SMART Security Cooperation Objectives: Improving DoD Planning and Guidance*, Santa Monica, Calif.: RAND Corporation, RR-1430-OSD, 2016. As of May 4, 2022: https://www.rand.org/pubs/research_reports/RR1430.html

NATO—*See* North Atlantic Treaty Organization.

NATO DEEP—*See* NATO Defense Education Enhancement Program.

NATO Defense Education Enhancement Program, *Institutional Capacity Building PME Bi-Monthly Report*, Brussels, January–February 2020a.

NATO Defense Education Enhancement Program, *Institutional Capacity Building PME Bi-Monthly Report*, Brussels, March–April 2020b.

NATO Defense Education Enhancement Program, provider email correspondence with program managers, April 2020c.

North Atlantic Treaty Organization, "Defence and Related Security Capacity Building Initiative," Brussels, June 9, 2021.

North Atlantic Treaty Organization, "Partners," webpage, March 27, 2020. As of May 4, 2022: https://www.nato.int/cps/en/natohq/51288.htm

North Atlantic Treaty Organization International Staff, *2019 DEEP Events Report for Tunisia*, unpublished, 2019a.

North Atlantic Treaty Organization International Staff, *Defence Education Enhancement Programme (DEEP) Key Facts and Procedures*, NATO Notice AC/340-N (2020)0092 (R), June 15, 2019b.

North Atlantic Treaty Organization International Staff, "Report on the 9th Clearing House on Defence Education Held Online, 14-22 September 2020," AC/340-N(2020)0054 (R), October 6, 2020, pp. 1–15.

North Atlantic Treaty Organization Newsroom, "NATO Defence Education Enhancement Programme (DEEP) Deepens Defence Capacity Building for Partners," September 25, 2020a.

North Atlantic Treaty Organization Newsroom, "NATO Defence Education Enhancement Programme (DEEP) Supports Distance Learning in Response to the COVID-19 Pandemic," November 24, 2020b.

Office of the Under Secretary of Defense for Policy, *DoD Instruction 5132.14: Assessment, Monitoring, and Evaluation Policy for the Security Cooperation Enterprise*, Washington, D.C., U.S. Department of Defense, January 13, 2017.

Oliker, Olga, Lynn E. Davis, Keith Crane, Andrew Radin, Celeste Ward Gventer, Susanne Sondergaard, James T. Quinlivan, Stephan B. Seabrook, Jacopo Bellasio, Bryan Frederick, Andriy Bega, and Jakub Hlavka, *Security Sector Reform in Ukraine*, Santa Monica, Calif.: RAND Corporation, RR-1475-1-UIA, 2016. As of May 4, 2022: https://www.rand.org/pubs/research_reports/RR1475-1.html

Organization for Security and Co-operation in Europe, "New National Platform Fosters Inclusive Dialogue on Democratic Oversight of Security Sector in Armenia," Communications and Media Relations Section, OSCE Secretariat, February 27, 2020.

Ortiz, Chris A, *The Psychology of Lean Improvements: Why Organizations Must Overcome Resistance and Change the Culture*, London: Taylor & Francis, 2012.

Partnership for Peace Consortium, "Strategic Plan for DEEP Armenia for 2017," draft, December 31, 2016a.

Partnership for Peace Consortium, "Strategic Plan for DEEP Kazakhstan: 2017," unpublished, December 31, 2016b.

Partnership for Peace Consortium, "Strategic Plan for DEEP Armenia for 2018," draft, April 30, 2018.

Partnership for Peace Consortium, *SAC/CSC Meeting Minutes*, unpublished, November 19, 2019.

Partnership for Peace Consortium, "Strategic Plan for DEEP Kazakhstan: 2020-21," unpublished, March 29, 2020a.

Partnership for Peace Consortium, "Strategic Plan for DEEP Tunisia for 2020-21," unpublished, March 29, 2020b.

Partnership for Peace Consortium, "Strategic Plan for DEEP Armenia: 2020-21," draft, March 30, 2020c.

Partnership for Peace Consortium, *NATO Defense Education Enhancement Program Monitoring and Evaluation Analysis: 2020*, working paper, April 6, 2020d.

Partnership for Peace Consortium, "Strategic Plan for DEEP Ukraine 2020," unpublished, August 20, 2020e.

Partnership for Peace Consortium, "Strategic Plan for DEEP Armenia 2020," unpublished, October 20, 2020f.

Partnership for Peace Consortium, "Strategic Plan for DEEP Ukraine 2020," unpublished, October 22, 2020g.

Partnership for Peace Consortium, "Educator's Workshop and MIP Planning Schedule," working paper, October 23, 2020h.

Partnership for Peace Consortium, "PfP Educators Workshop and MIP Planning Schedules," working paper, October 23, 2020i.

Partnership for Peace Consortium and NATO International Staff, "Information Paper: Reference Curricula Available for DEEP Utilization, unpublished, June 2020.

Partnership for Peace Consortium Education Development Working Group, "Measures of Effectiveness (MOE) for the Defense Education Enhancement Program (DEEP)," unpublished, December 31, 2016.

Partnership for Peace Consortium Education Development Working Group, "NATO Defense Education Enhancement Program (DEEP) August 2019–August 2020 Monitoring and Evaluation Analysis," working paper, March 30, 2020a.

Partnership for Peace Consortium Education Development Working Group, *Faculty Development Programs Overview*, briefing, December 2020b.

Partnership for Peace Consortium Education Development Working Group, "EDWG Input for the 2020 Annual PfPC Report," working paper, December 10, 2020c.

Partnership for Peace Consortium Education Development Working Group Educators Faculty Development Group, "Faculty Development Programs Fact Sheet," unpublished, September 5, 2021.

Perepelitsa, Grigoriy, "The Development of Civil-Military Relations in Post-Soviet Ukraine," in Andrew Cottey, Timothy Edmunds, and Anthony Forster, eds., *Democratic Control of the Military in Postcommunist Europe: Guarding the Guards*, London: Palgrave MacMillan, 2002, pp. 233–247.

PfPC—*See* Partnership for Peace Consortium.

PfPC EDWG—*See* Partnership for Peace Consortium Education Development Working Group.

Santini, Ruth Hanau and Giulia Cimini, "The Politics of Security Reform in Post-2011 Tunisia: Assessing the Role of Exogenous Shocks, Domestic Policy Entrepreneurs and External Actors," *Middle Eastern Studies*, Vol., 55, No. 2, 2019, pp. 225–241.

Solis, Mariusz, *Professional Military Education (PME) Development Under the Defence Education Enhancement Programme (DEEP), Annex 1: DEEP Ukraine 2020 Programme Review*, NATO Notice AC/340(NUC), June 15, 2020.

Stolberg, Alan G., "Institutional Capacity Building PME Bi-Monthly Report NATO Defense Education Enhancement Program (DEEP) Africa Military Education Program (AMEP)," unpublished, May–June 2020a.

Stolberg, Alan G., *Defence Education Enhancement Programme and Defence Education Enhancement Programme Update*, briefing to the NATO Partnerships and Cooperative Security Committee, December 10, 2020b.

Stolberg, Alan G., Stuart E. Johnson, and Lura Kupe, *Building Partner-Nation Capacity Through the Defense Education Enhancement Program*, Santa Monica, Calif.: RAND Corporation, PE-286-OSD, 2018. As of May 4, 2022:
https://www.rand.org/pubs/perspectives/PE286.html

Terhart, Ewald, "Teacher Resistance Against School Reform: Reflecting an Inconvenient Truth," *School Leadership & Management*, Vol. 33, No. 5, 2013, pp. 486–500.

Urbelis, Vaidotas, and Tomas Urbonas, "The Challenges of Civil-Military Relations and Democratic Control of Armed Forces: The Case of Lithuania," in Andrew Cottey, Timothy Edmunds, and Anthony Forster, eds., *Democratic Control of the Military in Postcommunist Europe: Guarding the Guards*, London: Palgrave MacMillan, 2002, pp 108–125.